Linguistics

THE BOBBS-MERRILL SERIES IN *Speech Communication*
RUSSEL R. WINDES, *Editor*
Queens College of the City University of New York

PETER H. SALUS

Scarborough College
University of Toronto

Linguistics

The Bobbs-Merrill Company, Inc.
INDIANAPOLIS AND NEW YORK

FOR W. H. AUDEN

ACKNOWLEDGMENTS

The problems in Chapters I and II are from the **Workbook in Descriptive Linguistics** by Henry Allen Gleason, Jr. (New York: Holt, Rinehart, and Winston, Inc., 1955) and are reprinted with permission of the publisher.

The author would like to thank Gary L. Bevington, Mrs. Mary Greenwood, and James E. Cathey (all of the University of Massachusetts), Michael C. Shapiro (of the University of Chicago), and Paul M. Postal (of the International Business Machines Company) for their comments and assistance.

Special thanks is due to Russel R. Windes, the editor of this series, for his encouragement.

Editor's foreword

The study of language was, until recent times, the province of humanistic scholars in the university, seminary, and academy. The hallmark of the learned was a knowledge of rhetoric and an acquaintance with tongues both antique and modern. Consequently, the most esteemed professors mastered language, its origin and development, its structure, and its use in literature and public address. This concentration on language made the professor a man at once revered and mocked: revered for his competence in Hebrew, Greek, Latin, German and Sanskrit, and his knowledge of Homer, Horace, Cicero, Quintillian and Alcuin; mocked because his erudition had so little relevance to practical affairs. However, practical affairs are now, for better and worse, firmly in the saddle, and the professor, if he is to be esteemed, is spurred onward by practical social needs. More precisely, the line between scholarship and the practical has been erased—the scholar has become preeminently the practical man.

Three forces have worked together to change the course of the study of language: the demands which society now places on knowledge; the influence of the social sciences; and basic changes in our educational purposes. Just as the professor of chemistry no longer seeks to produce gold, but gets gold to produce new medicines (and new diseases for chemical warfare), so the humanistic professor no longer seeks to mystify the general public, but to enlighten the public mind. Extending

vii

the analogy further, just as the physical scientist no longer sees the natural world as an object of observation and speculation, but an uncertain reality to be manipulated, so the humanistic professor now sees language as a tool to be analyzed, employed and modified. Here the analogy ends, for other forces must enter. Language has become a subject for social scientists: as an artifact of culture; as a reflection of popular consciousness; as a means of influence. No longer, then can the student of language be merely decorative. He must answer questions, within his competence, posed by social scientists and technicians. Beyond the drive toward practicality, and a vital connection with social science, language study has been transformed by changed conceptions of education. With the American commitment to make every man an intellectual, the need has arisen to show every man the nature of language, and its place in intellectual life. Concomitant with this need is the compulsion to reduce subjects once reserved by their very complexity to the few, to the relative simplicities of the many. One element of the study of language is linguistics, and it is the applicable essence of this subject which Professor Salus seeks here to communicate.

Linguistics is the study of language as a human phenomenon. At the present time, linguistic study is following two paths: descriptive linguistics, which is concerned with the segmentation and classification of human speech: and transformational-generative grammar which seeks to explicate utterances in order to comprehend just how original sentences are created and understood.

In this book, Professor Salus begins by describing the basic concepts of descriptive linguistics. He then moves to a discussion of transformational-generative grammar. The student thus obtains a basic view of language study in the mid-twentieth century.

This volume is, of course, introductory, and not exhaustive. Since the student may be interested in fields allied to linguistics, Professor Salus goes beyond the central concerns of linguistics and discusses sociolinguistics, psycholinguistics and anthropological linguistics. His classified bibliography might guide study in any of these areas. Through this volume, then, students of communication, communicative disorders, and the social sciences will meet the basic concepts of linguistics, and receive help in further reading.

Russel R. Windes

Contents

Introduction

Linguistics is the study of language. This may seem tautologous, but the common confusion of a linguist with a polyglot, one who knows several (many) languages is sufficient reason for beginning with such a statement. Furthermore, the goals of such a study must be made explicit, for linguistics is not philology.

Philology is interested in language as a tool to enable the investigator to gain access to the literature, sociology, anthropology, history of the speakers of the language; frequently, the philologist is interested in literatures and cultures where the language is no longer spoken. In these cases he is involved with the written, etched, engraved, or printed word, but not with the spoken language.

The linguist is interested in the language for its own sake; or in language as a phenomenon of human behavior.

The essence of language is speech and the psychological realities underlying it; writing is merely secondary. In view of the fact that speech (sound) is transitory, we are reduced to using writing systems to represent it: most scholarship is eye-oriented, not ear-oriented.

The formal study of language began in ancient Greece, but linguistics as we know it today had its start in the late eighteenth century. In the past decade or so—especially in this country—linguistics has travelled along two paths, usually called descriptive linguistics and transformational-generative grammar. While attempting to cover the most important points of both of these approaches, this book will lean more to the latter "school."

On the most superficial level, the differences between these approaches may be summed up with the statement that whereas traditional American descriptivism sees language as a series of concatenations—of sounds into forms and of forms into larger syntactic entities, transformational-generative grammar sees the sentence—the unit utterance—as basic. The elaboration of the differences between these schools will be reserved for later.

Descriptions of languages—grammars—are of varying degrees of adequacy. Generally, three levels of adequacy are distinguished:

1. observational adequacy, where the grammar presents the observed primary data correctly;
2. descriptive adequacy, where the grammar gives a correct account of the linguistic intuition of the native speaker and specifies the observed data in terms of significant generalizations underlying regularities of the language; and
3. explanatory adequacy, where the linguistic theory associated with the grammar provides a basis for selecting that grammar which achieves descriptive adequacy over others which achieve observational adequacy. In this case, we might say that the linguistic theory supplies an explanation for the linguistic intuition of the native speaker.

Moreover, it is important to recognize that there are such things as language universals—facts about language in general, rather than facts about individual languages like English, Chinese, or Swahili. For example, every language consists of a set of sentences; and in every human language this set of sentences is infinite. The truth of this is easily demonstrated. The following are all well-formed English sentences:

1. Alvin's favorite number is one.
2. Alvin's favorite number is two.
3. Alvin's favorite number is three.
   And so on.

As are:

4. Alice dreamt she was a fishwife.
5. Alice dreamt she was a salesgirl.

6. Alice dreamt she was a telephone.

7. Alice dreamt she was a textbook.

There is no limit to the number of sentences that can be produced in this way, the only limit being the number of numbers (in the case of sentences 1–3) or the number of things Alice can dream of being (in sentences 4–7).

Some sentences are like others. Thus:

8. Irving sailed to Sweden in a coracle.

is more like:

9. Sam went to the drive-in in a car.

than it is like:

10. Sally hit her husband with the **St. Louis Post-Dispatch.**

This is because though there are an infinite number of sentences in any language, regularities underly them. This means that there are generalizations which can be made to explain sentence structure. These generalizations can be expressed as rules, and the total set of these rules (the set of generalizations underlying the structure of a language) is called the grammar of that language. We will look at the types of these rules and the forms they must take in Chapter Three, but first we will examine the traditional methods of analyzing the sound-system and form-system of a language.

Linguistics

ONE

The sounds of language

The organs of speech

The organs involved in producing speech sounds are the lungs, the windpipe, the larynx, the pharynx, the nose, and the mouth. These organs form a channel from the lungs to the lips. The part of this channel lying above the larynx—the pharynx, the mouth and the nose—is called the vocal tract, and its shape can be varied extensively by motion of the tongue, lips, and other parts of the anatomy.

Impetus for speech production comes from the stream of air which we exhale from the lungs. Normally, this is noiseless, but we can produce sound by setting this stream into vibration. There are several ways of effecting this vibration, but the most common is the use of the vocal cords, which are part of the larynx.

These cords are bands of cartilage running horizontally front to back across the trachea or windpipe. When these bands are open, the air stream passes unimpeded; when they are tightly closed, the air stream is closed off; and when they are partially shut, the air stream sets them in motion. The vibration of these bands of cartilage is called voice, and speech sounds incorporating this articulation are called voiced. The space between the vocal cords is called the glottis.

Basically, there are only two other methods for producing speech sounds: constriction of the vocal tract and closure of the vocal tract.

Those sounds produced by constricting the vocal tract at some point are called fricatives, the air stream at the point of constriction

3

becoming turbulent, like steam escaping from the narrow nozzle of a tea kettle.

The sounds produced by closure of the vocal tract are called stops or plosives. The pharynx is the part of the vocal tract immediately above the glottis. Basically, it is a tube connecting the larynx with the mouth and the nose.

The nasal cavity runs from the nostrils to the back of the mouth, where it can be separated from the mouth and the remainder of the pharynx by the elevation of the soft palate. We will discuss the soft palate later in this section.

We now come to the mouth, the most important part of the vocal tract. The shape of the mouth can be extensively altered through movement of the palate, the tongue, the teeth, and the lips—or rather the movement of some of these in relation to the others.

The tongue is the most moveable of these, as it can be moved front, back, up, or down. The lips can be rounded or spread, they may contact the teeth, or they may be closed completely to stop the air stream.

The teeth can be used to restrict the air stream in various ways, contacting the lips or the tongue.

Finally, the palate is divided into three parts: the alveolar ridge, the ridge just behind your front teeth; the bony hard palate along the roof of your mouth; and the muscular soft palate behind it. All of the sounds of English are produced with these organs.

The sounds of English

If we assemble a list of English words like:

pill	till	kill	chill
bill	dill	gill	Jill
mill	nil	fill	ville
will	Lil	sill	hill
rill			

you will note that they are identical, except for their initial sounds. If we put together another list like:

pet			Chet
bet	debt	get	jet
met	net		vet
wet	let	set	het
	yet		

we find that whereas there are some slots we cannot fill (there is no English word *ket [an asterisk before a word or sentence means that it is hypothetical or ungrammatical]), there is also an item which did not appear on our first list (there is no *yill in English).

If we pattern these words in pairs, like **pill:bill** or **wet:yet,** we can demonstrate that the difference between the first sound in each word is relevant to the sound pattern of English. When these words differ in only one sound, we refer to them as minimal pairs. A minimal pair demonstrates the relevance of a sound distinction in a language. The first list illustrates seventeen consonantal distinctions in English, and the second list, fourteen. But the second list also adds a sound to our inventory: **y-.**

We do not have to use initial sounds to demonstrate relevance or establish a minimal pair; we might set up sequences like **bill:bell:bull: ball** or **hit:hid:hip:his:hiss.** We have used initials for the sake of convenience.

In descriptive terms, the smallest relevant sound of a language is a phoneme, and we refer to the distinctions between **pill** and **bill** and **debt** and **get** as phonemic. The difference between the initial sound of **key** and that of **cow** or the one between the "k" sounds of **key** and **ski** is not relevant in English, and is therefore called non-phonemic or phonetic. However, they are different from one another in that the "k" of **key** is articulated further toward the front of the mouth than that of **cow,** and the one of **ski** has less force behind it than that of **key.** These differences are, however, automatic—initial **p, t,** and **k** are pronounced with greater force than those following other consonants. Pairs like **pill:spill, talk:stalk,** and **cool:school** illustrate this.

It is important to note here that sounds are phonemic or non-phonemic only in relationship to specific languages. In Hindi, for example, the distinction between the "k" sound in **key** and that of **ski** is most relevant, and in Arabic that between the "k" sound of **key** and that of **cow** is important.

It must be obvious that referring to sounds as "the 'k' sound of key" or "the initial sound of key" is rather cumbersome. As a result, people who are interested in sounds, use a set of symbols to specify just what they mean. In this symbolism, phonemes are enclosed in slash marks / /, the phonetic symbols are enclosed in brackets [ ]. Most consonants are represented by their alphabetic symbols. Thus, the consonants of English may be represented by the following set:

SYMBOL	INITIAL OCCURRENCE	FINAL OCCURRENCE
/p/	paste	rope
/b/	baste	robe
/t/	tot	feet
/d/	dot	feed
/k/	kale	lack
/g/	gale	lag
/f/	ferry	knife
/v/	very	knive
/m/	moon	loom
/n/	noon	loon
/ŋ/	—	long
/r/	rope	poor
/l/	lope	pool
/w/	wet	—
/y/	yet	—
/θ/	thigh	bath
/ð/	thy	bathe
/č/	cheap	catch
/ǰ/	jeep	cadge
/s/	sow	bass
/š/	show	bash
/z/	zoo	close
/ž/	—	rouge
/h/	hill	—

/ŋ/ never occurs initially. /ž/ only occurs initially in a few foreign words and names, like Zhukov. /h/ never occurs finally; nor do /w/ or /y/ in this material. There are thus 24 consonantal phonemes in English. Looking back at the acoustic information at the beginning of this chapter, we might classify these consonants as follows, based on their method of production. (See chart on page 7.)

There are, of course, many other sounds used in other languages, and a number of other symbols used to represent them. Thus we can write a raised ʰ after a stop to indicate an additional puff of air, called aspiration (the initial /k/ of **key** might be written [kʰ], for example). Small hooks beneath letters mean that they are articulated further forward, e.g. [ḳ] for a palatal /k/. Circles beneath usually voiced sounds denote voicelessness, e.g. [m̥] or [w̥]. Finally, [ȼ] is fre-

	BILABIAL	LABIODENTAL	DENTAL	ALVEOLAR	ALVEOPALATAL	VELAR	GLOTTAL
STOPS							
Voiced	b			d		g	
Voiceless	p			t		k	
AFFRICATES							
Voiced					ǰ		
Voiceless					č		
FRICATIVES							
Voiced		v	ð	z	ž		
Voiceless		f	θ	s	š		h
RESONANTS							
Lateral							
Voiced				l			
Nasal							
Voiced	m			n		ŋ	
Median							
Voiced	w			r	y		

quently used to represent [ts], as in English **hats;** and the voiceless glottal stop is indicated by [ʔ].

We can use the principle of minimal pairs to set up a set of vowels for English, too. Thus a series like:

bit	bet	bat	beat	bait	bout
boat	boot	but	bought	bite	bot

will establish that there are 12 "vowels" which occur between /b/ and /t/ and are distinctive in English. If we attempt to order these twelve yet more, we discover that **bit** and **beat** seem to have something in common; that is, the beginning of the vowel sound in **beat** is something like that of **bit.** When we compare **bet** and **bait,** we note that here, too, the beginning of the vowel of the latter is like that of the former. Furthermore, there is something similar about the last part of the vowels of **beat** and **bait**—and we can add the vowel of **bite** to this list also. Finally, we note that there is something which the last parts of the vowels of **bout, boat,** and **boot** have in common. We customarily consider the vowels of **bit, bet, bot, bat,** and **but** as being fundamental, and the vowels of the other words as having some additional component. This component is called a glide, and the resulting pair of sounds is called a diphthong. Descriptivists usually say that English has either two or three glides: /y/, /w/, and /H/, as well as nine vowels. As these vowels can either occur alone or with any of the glides, we might hypothesize 36 vowel sounds for English. Luckily, no dialect of English makes use of most of these possibilities. By and large, the following are sufficient to describe most varieties of the language:

/i/	bit	/iy/	beat				
/e/	bet	/ey/	bait				
/a/	bot	/ay/	bite	/aw/	bout		
/o/				/ow/	boat		
/u/	book			/uw/	boot	/uH/	tour
/æ/	bat	/æ/	maid			/æH/	salve
/ə/	but						
/ɨ/	children						
/ɔ/	cot	(in New England)					

Triangles and trapezoids are frequently used to represent schematically the position of the tongue in the production of vowels. When the tongue is near the palate we speak of close vowels, when the tongue is at the bottom of the mouth we speak of open vowels. We also speak of "front" and "back" vowels, depending on the position of the tongue. (Many languages, like German and French, distinguish between rounded and unrounded vowels, depending on the shape of the lips. Thus German [ü] is the rounded equivalent of [i], and [ö] of [e]. Rounding is not relevant in English.) Plotted on a quadrilateral, the vowels of English look as follows:

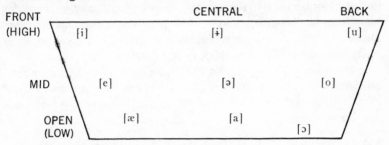

Such things as pitch, stress, and intonation are also relevant in most languages. In some languages, like Chinese, tones also play a role. We will not go into detail concerning these in this book. However, another phenomenon called juncture is of interest.

Juncture is the result of several different phonological phenomena, not the least of which is what might best be described as "pause." Juncture can be best demonstrated in such pairs as:

giant's eyes	giant size
Mikey's	my keys
candlesticks	(the) candle sticks

In each of these we note that there is a greater hiatus between the "words" in each item in the right hand column than there is on the left. This longer pause is called "open" juncture and is usually indicated by a plus sign (e.g., my + keys). "Close" juncture is usually unmarked: **giant size.**

Phonological analysis

In doing an analysis of a sound system, the concept of complementary distribution is quite useful. By complementary distribution, we mean that the phonetic system of the language is such that certain sounds never occur in the same environment. Thus, [kʰ] and [k] in English are in complementary distribution, for [kʰ] occurs only initially, and [k] never occurs initially. We thus say that [kʰ] and [k] are in complementary distribution, and that they form the allophones of one phoneme, /k/. A phoneme is a hypothetical construct. Only the allophones really occur. The phoneme is thus realized through its allophones.

In English, [ŋ] and [h] are in complementary distribution of a sort, for [ŋ] never occurs initially, and [h] never occurs finally. We consider them separate phonemes, however, because they lack another criterion: phonetic similarity. They are dissimilar in that [ŋ] is a voiced, velar nasal, whereas [h] is a voiceless, glottal fricative.

In the following list of words from Korean [l] and [r] are in complementary distribution and form one phoneme. Examine the material carefully and see if you can state the distribution. /ɨ/ is a high back unrounded vowel.

1. kal	that'll go	8. ilkop	seven	15. irɨmi	name
2. kɨnɨl	shade	9. ipalsa	barber	16. kiri	road
3. mul	water	10. onɨlppam	tonight	17. kɨrəm	then
4. pal	leg	11. pulpʰyən	discomfort	18. kəriro	to the street
5. pʰal	arm	12. silkwa	fruit	19. saram	person
6. səul	Seoul	13. tɨlcʰaŋ	window	20. uri	we
7. tatɨl	all of them	14. əlmana	how much	21. yərɨm	summer

As you know that [l] and [r] are in complementary distribution, the first thing you must do is examine the environments in which they occur. In items 1–7, [l] always occurs post-vocalically in final position. In items 8–14, [l] occurs post-vocalically and pre-consonantally. In 15–21, [r] always occurs intervocalically between vowels. Neither [l] nor [r] seems to occur initially. We can thus state our findings as follows:

[l] and [r] form one phoneme and are in complementary distribution. The distribution is:
    [l] occurs finally and pre-consonantally
    [r] occurs intervocalically.

Let us look at another list of words, this time from Totonac, a Mexican Indian language.

1.	¢apsḁ	he stacks	7. snapapḁ	white
2.	¢ilinksḁ	it resounded	8. stapu̥	beans
3.	kasitti̥	cut it	9. šumpi̥	porcupine
4.	kuku̥	uncle	10. taaqhu̥	you plunged in
5.	lkakḁ	peppery	11. tihašli̥	he rested
6.	miki̥	snow	12. tukšli̥	it broke

Here [ḁ i̥ u̥] are voiceless vowels in complementary distribution with their voiced counterparts, forming three phonemes /a i u/. The distribution is an obvious one: all final vowels are devoiced. It might be noted that every voiceless vowel in this corpus follows a voiceless consonant, and the question as to whether or not this voiceless consonant causes the devoicing of the vowel might arise. The answer here is quite simple. If we glance through the corpus, we must see that in nearly every item there are voiced vowels which follow voiceless consonants. If the preceding consonant had an influence on the following vowel, this could not be the case, and so we must conclude that it is the final position which causes the devoicing.

TWO

The form system of English

General remarks

The study of the sounds of language is usually called phonology. The study of the forms of language is morphology. Just as descriptivists consider the phoneme the basic significant unit of the sound system, they call the smallest meaningful units of a language **morphemes.** A morpheme is usually a sequence of phonemes, though it may be only a phoneme in length. Not every sequence of phonemes is a morpheme, however. The sequence [grib] is not a morpheme in English, for it lacks meaning. It is a **morph,** for it is a pronounceable sequence of sounds which might conceivably be added to the morpheme inventory of English, as **schmoo** and **kodak** and **radar** were added. A sequence like [pzklfsr] is neither a morph nor a morpheme, for it is not pronounceable in English. (This does not mean that no speaker of English can utter it; it means that the "permitted order" of sounds in English does not provide for a sequence like [pzk-], much less [pzklfsr].)

If a morpheme is a minimum meaningful unit, then it cannot be further divided without destruction or serious alteration of its meaning. **Porch** is a morpheme, for if we further divide its phonemes the resulting fragments bear no discernible relation to the meaning of **porch.** Many morphemes, like **porch,** contain one syllable: **boy, chair, star, -ing, -ness, -ly, pre-, un-.** Others are polysyllables: **elephant, Saskatchewan, language.** Still others are less than one syllable, like the **-s** of **hats.** Here both **hat** and **-s** are morphemes, for they both carry meaning. It must be pointed out that many morphemes are not words: in a word like **ungentlemanly,** the form is the result of gradual accretions of morphemes. **Un- + gentlemanly, gentleman + ly, gentle + man.**

Morphological devices

Just as phonemes embrace variants called allophones, morphemes have variants called allomorphs. However, where the phoneme is actualized only through its allophones, most morphemes are invariant, not depending on context or environment: **Alaska, -hood, -ing.** A good example of a morpheme with allomorphic variants, is the English plural, **-s.** This is realized as [s] in **hats,** as [z] in **heads,** and as [ɨz] in **roses.** Despite the differences in pronunciation, English speakers recognize that these forms are "the same," and in the case of literate speakers, spelling aids this identification. But most speakers are unaware of the places where they pronounce **-s** [s], [z] or [ɨz]. Investigation of a large body of material will demonstrate that the three forms occur in well-defined, mutually exclusive domains: the /ɨz/ forms are pronounced only after the final sounds of such words as **hiss, rose, bush, garage, match,** and **ledge** (/s z š ž č ǰ/), neither /s/ nor /z/ are found after these sounds; /-s/ occurs after the finals of **hip, rat, fork, cuff,** and **faith** (/p t k f θ/); and /-z/ occurs after all vowels and those consonants not covered by /-s/ and /-ɨz/. For the consonants, we have the final sounds of **cub, head, leg, stove, lathe, home, pin, ring, pole,** and **car.** Thus, allomorphs are in complementary distribution.

It must be noted that without knowing the facts about the distribution, the native speaker automatically selects the correct form. He does not hesitate in selecting the pertinent allomorph even if he is called upon to pluralize a word for the first time. A child has no second thoughts in choosing the right plural form for **bazooka, phoneme, psychopath,** or **beatnik,** and he has no second thoughts because allomorphs are automatic positional variants of morphemes.

/s/, /z/, and /ɨz/ qualify as allomorphs of the plural morpheme of English because they have the same meaning and are in complementary distribution. Forms like **peer** (noun) and **peer** (verb) are not allomorphs because, though they are identical phonetically, they lack the requirement of identity of meaning.

Allomorphs like those of the English plural morpheme are said to be phonologically conditioned; that is, in these cases the phonological nature of the form of the plural used depended on the phonetic character of the final sound of the singular. However, there are a number of other ways of forming the plural in English. These methods are called morphologically conditioned, and here there is no traceable phonological connection between the singular and the type of plural used. Examples of this are **ox:oxen, child:children,** and **sheep:sheep.** This last is an example of a zero form. Despite the seeming artificiality of this, it proves to be a most practical device for the description of many phenomena in many languages. **Sheep** is a plural when it occurs in the same environment in which forms like **dogs** and **horses** occur: **dogs run, horses run, sheep run.** This is a syntactic test, in which we set up an equation like **dog:dogs = sheep:sheep,** demonstrating that a zero ending takes the place of an inflection. There are other types of plurals in English, too: **man:men, mouse:mice, goose:geese,** and so on. It is the task of morphological analysis to describe their formation in a statement that will include all of the types of plurals mentioned in as neatly unified and economical a statement as possible.

Morphology also includes all the phenomena to which traditional grammar gives the names declension, conjugation, etc. In English, morphology includes paradigms, despite their limited scope when compared to some other languages. The English noun, for example, has the paradigm **book, book's, books, books'**—which is not exactly highly diversified. In the present tense, the verb is inflected for the third person singular **(writes, jumps).** The verb also differentiates the present and the past **(write:wrote).** Again, this is not a very diverse pattern. The traditional "parts of speech" are often determined on the basis of inflection: a verb, we say, is inflected for person, number and tense; a pronoun for person, number and case—but not (in English) for tense. Most English words are, of course, uninflected and must therefore be classified solely on a syntactic basis. The descriptivist view of morphology cannot deal with unaltering forms.

Affixes are morphological devices which occur widely. Affixes are morphemes like **-ed, -ing, pre-,** or **un-.** When they are added to the beginning of a word they are called prefixes, when they are attached to the end of a word, suffixes. A third type of affix (which does not occur in English) is the infix, which is inserted into the middle of a word or root. Infixation occurs in the present tense in Latin, for example, in **tango (ta-n-go)** 'I touch,' where the nasal infix is absent in other forms **(tetegi, tactus).**

A type of morpheme that plays an important role in English is the replacive, as in **sing:sang, goose:geese, man:men,** where a portion of the word is actually replaced by something else. The extreme case of replacement is called a suppletive, where the entire form is replaced: **go:went, be:was,** or, in Latin, **fero:ferre:tuli:latus.**

There are a number of types of morphological change. One of these types is assimilation. The **m** in **impossible** is an example of this, for here the negative prefix **in-** takes on the variant form **im-,** the dental nasal "changing" to a bilabial nasal under the influence of the following bilabial consonant. We call this regressive assimilation because of the direction of change. The assimilation is partial because the **n** has not become a **p.** In Latin **apporto** from **ad + porto,** we have an instance of total regressive assimilation. Progressive assimilation also occurs, as does non-contiguous assimilation, in which the altered sound and the cause of the alteration are not adjacent.

Such phenomena as umlaut in German and vowel harmony in Turkish and Hungarian are instances of non-contiguous (distant) assimilation. In Turkish, for example, there are four allomorphs for the suffix 'in': /-te -de -ta -da/. The forms with **-e** are used after words containing front vowels, these with **-a** after words with back vowels. The forms with **-d-** are used with words ending in a voiced sound, and those with **-t-** with words ending in voiceless sounds. Thus we have:

Bebek-te	'in the town of Bebek'
ev-de	'in the house'
yatak-ta	'in bed'
oda-da	'in the room'

Morphological analysis

The following data are from Luganda, a language of Uganda. Analyze the affixes.

1.	omukazi	woman	abakazi	women
2.	omusawo	doctor	abasawo	doctors
3.	omusika	heir	abasika	heirs
4.	omuwala	girl	abawala	girls
5.	omulenzi	boy	abalenzi	boys

It should be apparent that we are here dealing with a prefix, or rather, two prefixes: **omu-** which indicates 'one-ness' or singular, **aba-** which indicates plurality. Were we now given a word /omuntu/ 'person,' we would assume that the Luganda word for people is /abantu/—and we would be correct. But see what happens when we look at some more data:

6.	omuti	tree	emiti	trees
7.	omudumu	jug	emidumu	jugs
8.	omusumaali	nail	emisumaali	nails
9.	olunaku	day	ennaku	days
10.	olusenyi	plain	ensenyi	plains
11.	ekintu	thing	ebintu	things
12.	ekibbo	basket	ebibbo	baskets

Here, items 6–8 seem to have **omu-/emi-,** 9 and 10 **olu-/en-,** and 11 and 12 **eki-/ebi-** for their singular and plural prefixes. 1–5, as we noted, have **omu-/aba-.** What we see here is that Luganda has a number of noun classes, much like the gender classes of German, each of which has a different set of singular and plural prefixes. Items 1–5 were all persons, and we might thus correct our first statement by noting that **omu-/aba-** indicate singular and plural when the noun is human.

In the preceding two chapters we have attempted to give a brief view of the methods and scope of American descriptive linguistics. In the next chapter, we will look at the methodology and approach of the most recent "school" of linguistic analysis and description—transformational-generative grammar.

THREE

The nature of grammatical rules

Introduction

The grammar of a language enumerates or generates the sentences of that particular language. It does this by means of a finite number of rules, called **grammatical rules.** These grammatical rules must fulfill certain requirements. These are:

1. The rules must be **explicit:** that is, when applied, these must make clear the relationships between the elements of the various sentences they produce; the rules must be formulated in such a way that the personal inclinations of the user are irrelevant. The rules must, therefore, be self-explanatory.
2. The rules must be **formal:** the units in which the rules are expressed must be the real data of the language (the words, sounds, categories, etc). This formalness does not refer to the way in which the units are decided upon, but to the way in which they are used once analysis is complete.
3. The rules must be **complete:** they must account for all the facts of the language, but they must neither be too general nor too specific. (It must be obvious that grammatical rules never actually completely meet these criteria. Nevertheless, these are goals towards which a grammarian must strive. The success of a particular grammar is a function of the degree of complicity with these criteria.)

17

There are several types of restrictions which may be placed on grammatical rules. The type and degree of restriction must, of course, depend upon the language being described and the information we possess concerning language universals. If certain restrictions enable us to simplify our description of a given language, they must be used—the decision must be based upon the actualities, the facts of language structure.

One type of restriction is that of ordering some rules with regard to others or with each other. It may come to pass that two rules must occur in a specific sequence. When this is the case, the rules are said to be **ordered.** If only some rules, not all, are ordered with regard to others, the grammar is partially ordered. If the rules are arranged so that the first recurs after the last, the rules are cyclically ordered.

Another type of restriction concerns the environment in which a rule operates. If a rule operates on some sequence without regard for the environment of this sequence, the rules are **context-free.** If the operation of the rules is contingent upon the environment, the rules are **context-sensitive.**

Finally, rules may be obligatory or optional; that is, there are some rules which must take place, and others which may take place.

There are at least three types of rules required for the description of a natural language: **phrase structure** or **rewrite rules, transformational rules,** and **morphophonemic rules.**

Phrase structure rules. A grammar of a language consists of a number of rules which begin with a symbol and replace it with one or more other symbols. These may then be rewritten by other rules. Symbols which may not be rewritten are terminal symbols; those which must be rewritten are non-terminal symbols. Rewrite rules have the form:

$$A \rightarrow B + C \quad \text{or}$$

$$A \rightarrow b + c$$

where the arrow ($\rightarrow$) means "is rewritten as," A, B and C are non-terminal symbols, and b and c are terminal symbols. These phrase structure rules generate the set of deep structures of the language. It is the purpose of these structures to make explicit the meanings of the sentences with which they are associated. Each of these structures may be represented by a structural description which may in turn be of the form of a tree-diagram. Tree-diagrams are constructed by connecting the symbols on the left side of the rewrite rule to those on the right. Thus, from $A \rightarrow b + c$ we may derive:

Carrying on the process, every part of a structural description must be labelled in such a way that the components of the phrase structure rules are classified.

Deep structure

Traditional grammatical description broke sentences down into their component parts. These components were then classified as "parts of speech," on an inflectional and slot-and-filler basis. Under this system, a sentence like:

1. The brown moth swallowed Massachusetts.

would be said to consist of a noun phrase **the brown moth** and a verb phrase **swallowed Massachusetts.** The noun phrase in turn would be broken down into a definite article **the,** an adjective **brown,** and a noun **moth.** The verb phrase would be said to contain the verb **swallowed** and noun **Massachusetts. The brown moth** is the subject of the verb **swallowed** and **Massachusetts** is the object of the verb. The sentence:

2. Massachusetts was swallowed by the brown moth.

however, would be said to consist of a noun phrase **Massachusetts** and a verb phrase **was swallowed by the brown moth.** This verb phrase is composed of a verbal auxiliary **was,** a passive verb **swallowed,** and a prepositional phrase **by the brown moth.** The prepositional phrase is made up of a preposition **by** and the noun phrase **the brown moth,** which is composed of the denite article, the adjective and the noun. **Massachusetts** is the subject of **was swallowed** and **the brown moth** is the object of the preposition **by.**

If we compare the grammatical descriptions of sentences 1 and 2 with each other, we will note that except for the actual words (the moth was **brown,** not **blue**), the descriptions are dissimilar. The subjects, verbs, and objects are different. **Massachusetts** serves a different function in each sentence. Furthermore, this sort of description does not express a number of important generalizations about English. It is nowhere stated, for example, that in both cases it is **the brown moth** which is the agent of the action, nor that what is eaten is **Massachusetts.**

This sort of generalization is important because every speaker of English knows that, save for minor stylistic variations, the two sentences "mean" the same thing. It is a basic fact of English that sentences containing **Max threw** . . . and . . . **was thrown by Max** somehow express the same "logical" relationship between the subject and the verb. Any adequate grammar must capture this sort of generalization.

The transformational-generative approach to grammar attempts to do this through the presentation of two distinct levels of grammatical representation: deep structure and surface structure. A description of the surface structure of a sentence provides information as to the way that the sentence is manifested—the way that it is pronounced. The deep structure makes explicit what the sentence means, it reveals the logical relations between the elements of the sentence.

Thus, as sentences 1 and 2 **mean** the same thing, they are assigned identical deep structures. As they are pronounced differently, they have different surface structures. The deep structure and the surface structure are linked by **transformations,** rules which operate on deep structures, perform various operations, and produce thereby surface structures. Sentences 1 and 2 are derived from a common deep structure, and a simplified "tree diagram" of this structure would look like:

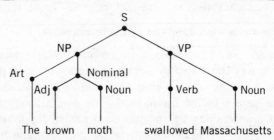

This deep structure is grossly over-simplified in many ways, but we shall ignore this fact. It does however satisfy the criteria set up at the beginning of this chapter: it is formal (only functional units of the language system—grammatical categories—are used); it is explicit (such relations as subject-verb are made apparent by the linear arrangement); and it is complete (the branchings illustrate the structural relationships). Moreover, we could generate this deep structure by a small number of phrase structure rules:

P.S.1.   S → NP + VP

P.S.2. NP → Article + Nominal
P.S.3. Nominal → Adj + Noun
P.S.4. VP → Verb + Noun
P.S.5. Art → **the**
P.S.6. Adj → **brown**
P.S.7. Noun → **moth** or **Massachusetts**
P.S.8. Verb → **swallowed**

These rules are both context-free and unordered as are all phrase structure rules.

The fact that the deep structure of sentences 1 and 2 looks much like the surface structure of sentence 1 is deceptive, for it might lead to the erroneous conclusion that sentence 2 is derived from sentence 1. The deep structure underlying both sentences is an abstract entity postulated to explicate the two sentences. In this case the generation of the surface form of sentence 2 required a transformation called the PASSIVE TRANSFORMATION. This transformation is not needed to generate the surface structure of sentence 1. The surface form of sentence 1 thus resembles the common deep structure more closely than does that of sentence 2. It is important to note, however, that the deep structure may resemble **none** of the surface structures derived from it.

The context-free, unordered phrase structure rules replace symbols on the left side of the arrow with symbols on the right side of the arrow until all the symbols on the right side are terminal symbols. The structures thus produced are deep structures which make explicit the relations between the elements of the sentence. Phrase structure rules are frequently said to make up the **base portion** of the grammar.

In rewrite rules we sometimes come across the situation in which symbol A is rewritten as B + C and symbol B, in turn, is rewritten as A + X. This type of rule produces such structures as:

As symbol A may again be rewritten as B + C, the process may be continued indefinitely. Rules which permit the reoccurrence of symbols already substituted for are called **recursive rules.** The fact that phrase structure rules are often recursive accounts for the fact that we can derive an infinite number of sentences from a finite number of rules.

On occasion, several phrase structure rules resemble one another closely enough that they can be collapsed into a single rule. Certain notational conventions have been adopted and we shall discuss these here. If the members of a set of rules all have the same symbol on the left side of the arrow, the various symbols on the right side of the arrow may be placed inside braces. Within the braces they may be ordered vertically or horizontally. If they are ordered horizontally, then they are separated by commas. In this way, we might rewrite P.S.7 as:

P.S.7a. $N \rightarrow \begin{Bmatrix} \text{moth} \\ \text{Massachusetts} \end{Bmatrix}$

or:

P.S.7b. $N \rightarrow \{ \text{moth, Massachusetts} \}$

Here the braces indicate that one, and only one, of the enclosed items must be chosen.

Similarly, we might have rules like:

P.S.9.   Verb Phrase $\rightarrow$ Verb

and:

P.S.10.   Verb Phrase $\rightarrow$ Verb + Noun

which could be rewritten as:

P.S.11.   Verb Phrase $\rightarrow$ Verb (+ Noun)

where the parentheses indicate that the enclosed symbols are optional; i.e., Verb Phrase may be rewritten as Verb or as Verb Noun. These notations may be combined. Thus the set of rules:

P.S.12a.   VP $\rightarrow$ Verb
P.S.12b.   VP $\rightarrow$ Verb + Noun Phrase
P.S.12c.   VP $\rightarrow$ Verb + Adverb

may be collapsed into:

P.S.12d. $VP \rightarrow \text{Verb} \left(+ \begin{Bmatrix} \text{Noun Phrase} \\ \text{Adverb} \end{Bmatrix} \right)$

In this way, a set of phrase structure rules which provides for all of the deep structures of a language may be constructed. We will set up some rules and see how they work later in this chapter.

Transformations

As was stated above, all natural languages have a set of grammatical rules called transformations which act upon deep structures to produce surface structures. In this section we will investigate this process.

Transformations can do more than can phrase structure rules. Rewrite rules replace single non-terminal symbols with one or more other symbols. Rewrite rules expand symbols into other symbols. Transformations do not have to operate on single symbols. Moreover, they may add or delete elements, change the order of elements, or substitute symbols—or any combination of these.

Unlike phrase structure rules, transformations are both context-sensitive and ordered. More than one transformation is required to generate a surface structure from any given deep structure. Each structure produced by the action of a transformation is a derived structure; and thus only the first of a series of transformations actually acts upon the deep structure, each successive transformation acting upon some derived structure. The derived structure produced by the last of a series of transformations is the surface structure. Every sentence generated thus has as many derived structures as transformations are used. This may be represented in the following way:

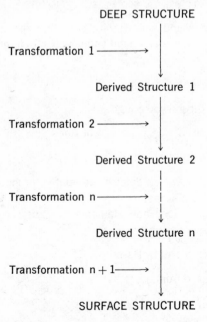

DEEP STRUCTURE

Transformation 1 ⟶

Derived Structure 1

Transformation 2 ⟶

Derived Structure 2

Transformation n ⟶

Derived Structure n

Transformation n + 1 ⟶

SURFACE STRUCTURE

Just as phrase structure rules are indicated with an arrow (→) transformations are indicated with a double arrow (⇒). Some of the most common transformations used in natural languages are deletion transformations. In these, some symbols appearing to the left of the double arrow are erased on the right side. English imperatives are the result of this transformation. A sentence like:

3. Close the door!

is derived from a deep structure having the form:

4. You close the door.

This sentence may seem strange because it does not resemble the surface form of any grammatical English utterance. But you must remember that deep structures are postulated entities which help us account for the behavior of sentences; and the fact that sentences like:

5. Close the door, won't you.
6. Close the door yourself.

and:

7. I want you to close the door.

all contain **you,** would seem to indicate that the deep structure of sentence 3 must have an element **you** which is deleted by a later transformation.

Similarly, the sentence:

8. Fred stole the gin you bought.

may be derived from:

9. Fred stole the gin which you bought.

by a transformation which deletes the relative pronoun **which** in some restrictive relative clauses.

Other transformations add elements to structures. Thus **by** is inserted into passive sentences:

10. The hat was burnt by Harpo.

is therefore derived from:

11. Harpo burnt the hat.

by means of a transformation which, among other things, inserts the preposition **by.**

Transformations also change the order of elements, as can be shown in English passives.

12. Pogo was assaulted by Churchy.

is derived from:

13. Churchy assaulted Pogo.

by a transformation which, in addition to inserting **by,** reverses the order of the two noun phrases. In the same way,

14. Sam threw the drunk out.

may be generated from:

15. Sam threw out the drunk.

by a transformation which moves the particle **out** of the verb **threw out** to a position after the noun phrase **the drunk.**

All of these transformations—and the many others which are a part of English grammar—must be formalized to be meaningful. As has been stated, the general form of these rules is that of a string of symbols followed by the double arrow ($\Rightarrow$), which is in turn followed by another string of symbols. The first string of symbols indicates the symbols to be operated upon by the transformation, as well as those symbols which are the rule's context. This string is the **input** to the transformation. The symbols to the right of the double arrow are the structures (or the symbols for the structures) resulting from the application of the transformation. When some forms are invariant in a given transformation, they are represented by symbols like mathematical variables in an algebraic equation. In the rule:

T.1.   X, noun, verb Y $\Rightarrow$ X, verb, noun, Y

X and Y can represent any symbols, or, possibly, nothing. What the rule states is that the noun and verb change places and that this change is not dependent upon what precedes or follows the noun and verb.

In order to make the notion of transformation less abstract, let us look at the PASSIVE TRANSFORMATION.

T.2.   X, Noun Phrase 1, Verb Phrase, Noun Phrase 2, Y $\Rightarrow$ X, Nou
phrase 2, be, passive form of verb, by $+$ Noun Phrase 1, Y

This transformation allows the generation of:

16.   Seven overripe plums were eaten by Hiawatha yesterday.

from:

17.   Hiawatha ate seven overripe plums yesterday.

Moreover, it involves both permutation and addition of elements.
does not matter at all what occupies the X and Y positions: both may t
filled, either may be empty, or both may be empty. The Passive Tran
formation will operate anyway. There are a large number of transform
tions in English, and rather than explicate all of them, we will mere
label and exemplify some of them here.

IDENTICAL NOUN PHRASE DELETION. The deep structure of a se
tence like:

18.   Sam adores to travel to Biloxi.

most likely contains structures similar to

19.   *Sam adores it [for Sam to travel to Biloxi].

The identical noun phrase deletion transformation deletes the repe
tion:

T.3.   *Sam adores it [for Sam to travel to Biloxi] $\Rightarrow$ Sam adores
travel to Biloxi.

EXTRAPOSITION. The extraposition transformation moves an er
bedded sentence:

T.4.   *it [that Spock is a great pediatrician] is true $\Rightarrow$ It is true th
Spock is a great pediatrician.

COMPLEMENTIZER DELETION. This transformation optionally d
letes a relative pronoun:

T.5.   We saw that the dog was awake $\Rightarrow$ We saw the dog was awak

"IT" DELETION.

T.6.   *it [that Spock is a great pediatrician] is true $\Rightarrow$ That Spock
a great pediatrician is true.

INDEFINITE NOUN PHRASE DELETION. This is most easily exemplified in conjunction with T.2 the passive transformation, as:

T.7.   passive
    Someone built the fort last week $\implies$ The fort was built by
                          indefinite NP deletion
    someone last week $\implies$ The fort was built
    last week.

RELATIVE CLAUSE. Relative clauses are the result of embedded sentences. We thus have a relative clause transformation, the results of which are as follows:

T.8. *the stork [the stork was lame] flew in circles $\implies$ The stork
    which was lame flew in circles.

ADJECTIVE TRANSFORMATION. Like relative clauses, adjectives are the result of sentence embedding. The basic notion here is that such constructions as **the red telephone** are the results of a transformation acting upon, for example, the telephone is red. Thus the adjective transformation also assumes a deletion of "be" or some form of it. This is usually referred to as the RELATIVE "BE" DELETION. A full sequence might look like this:

                                      T.8
          *the stork[the stork was lame] flew in circles $\implies$ The
    T.9   Relative "BE" deletion
          stork which was lame flew in circles $\implies$
    T.10.   adjective
          *the stork lame flew in circles $\implies$ The lame
          stork flew in circles.

There are also question and negation transformations, but we will not concern ourselves with them at this time. Let us rather look at some sentences and the ways in which they are represented by tree-diagrams.

20. Sam runs.

This is a simple sentence in which we have a noun phrase (NP) and a verb phrase (VP). This dichotomy is basic to every tree, though branchings with more than two limbs are possible. The tree that represents this sentence thus has the shape:

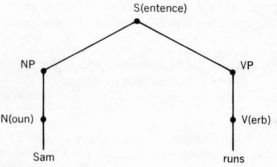

The sentence:

21. The house has a chimney.

has a tree like:

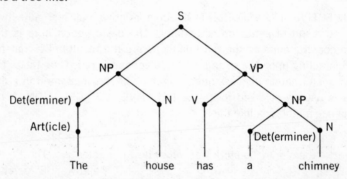

Note that here, as illustrated earlier, we have a verb phrase which contains a noun phrase. When a symbol lies immediately below another symbol on a tree-diagram, we say that the upper symbol **dominates** the lower symbol. In the diagram of sentence 21, S dominates another NP as provided for in P.S.12d. We say that the NP dominated by S is the deep subject of the sentence and that the NP dominated by the VP which is in turn dominated by S is the deep object. As we mentioned earlier, recursions are not only permissible, but frequent, and thus S may be embedded in an NP or a VP.

22. The small blue bird ate the large green bug.

has embeddings which, when expanded, would look like:

23. *The bird [the bird is small] [the bird is blue] ate
    the bug [the bug is large] [the bug is green].

and a deep structure tree of this would look like:

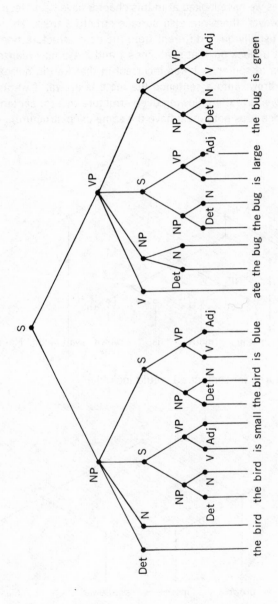

The trees we have looked at in this chapter have been deep structure trees. However, there are also surface structure trees. These surface trees are usually quite different from the deep structure trees. For example, let us look back at sentences 1 and 2. We now realize that the tree drawn of sentence 1 was incorrect in that we did not expand the adjective **brown** into a sentence **the moth is brown.** If we add this to our tree, we have the following deep structure tree for sentence 1 (and for sentence 2, as both must have the same deep structure):

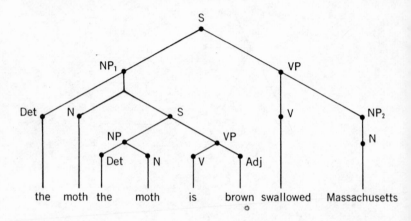

A surface tree for sentence 1 would look like:

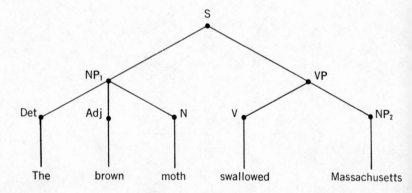

and a surface tree of sentence 2 would look like:

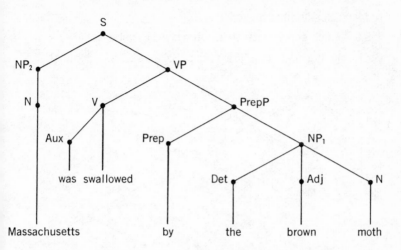

Thus we can immediately recognize the effects of the passive transformation, especially as the NPs have been numbered (see T.2).

Let us now take a sentence:

S.   Hobbits love ripe mushrooms.

and set up a series of phrase structure rules for it.

P.S.a. $S \rightarrow NP + VP$
P.S.b. $VP \rightarrow V + NP$
P.S.c. $NP \rightarrow (Adj +) N$
P.S.d. $V \rightarrow love$
P.S.e. $Adj \rightarrow ripe$
P.S.f. $N \rightarrow \begin{Bmatrix} hobbits \\ mushrooms \end{Bmatrix}$

These six rules could give us:

S.1.   Ripe hobbits love mushrooms.
S.2.   Mushrooms love ripe hobbits.
S.3.   Ripe mushrooms love hobbits.
S.4.   Hobbits love ripe mushrooms.

The last of which is the desired string, but all of which are certainly grammatical.

Let us now apply T.2 to string S.4:

S.5.   Ripe mushrooms are loved by hobbits.

Or let us expand the second NP (T.8):

S.6.   Mushrooms which are ripe are loved by hobbits.

Obviously, the deep structure trees of S.4 and S.5 are identical:

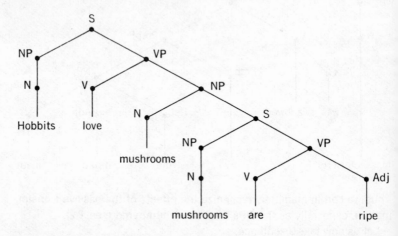

However, though the deep structure tree of S.6 would also be the same as the tree for S.4 and S.5, it might be necessary for us to indicate just which of these three logically equivalent sentences we were interested in. This can be effected by adding a branch or several branches to the top left of our tree, and indicating the transformations required. For example, the tree for S.6 might be redrawn as:

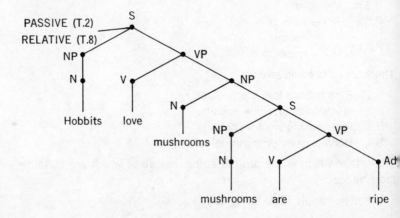

An analysis of the many sentences of English would provide us with a set of phrase structure rules which would supply all of the base components of English. These rules would presumably have access to a lexicon or dictionary which would have every entry listed with a series of features that "go together with" the lexical items—the word. We will look at such features on page 41, Chapter Four.

Morphophonemics

The third type of rules used in grammatical descriptions is the **morphophonemic rule.** The nature of these rules is far from obvious, but should become apparent with a little explication.

All of the structures discussed thus far in this chapter can be linearly represented by words. That is to say, the units out of which the utterances we have considered are composed, are well-formed English words. Admittedly we have oversimplified in this; frequently abstract markers, not words, are used. As such, the abstract markers have no phonological form, and the primary role of morphophonemic rules is to assign a phonological structure to these forms. Like transformations, morphophonemic rules are context-sensitive. The inputs to morphophonemic rules are surface structures and the outputs are phonological representations. This qualifies the earlier statement which said that the surface structure provides all the information necessary to pronounce the sentence it represents. What we can now say with confidence is that the surface structure serves as the input to the phonological apparatus, and that the output of these morphophonemic rules serves as the input to the actual vocal organs.

If we qualify parts of the tree structure we have used previously, we could represent sentence 1 by the following surface tree:

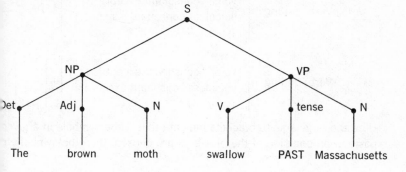

The morphophonemic rules of English operating upon this structure convert **swallow** + PAST to **swallowed;** they tell us that the PAST element is realized as **-d.** If the verb in this sentence had been **stalk,** the element PAST would not have been realized as [d] but as [t]. PAST is realized in several different ways, depending on the verb which precedes it. In the case of the so-called weak verbs, the PAST element is realized as [d], [t], or [ɨd]. In other verbs we find replacives **(sit:sat)** and suppletives **(go:went).** These varying forms must be predicted by the morphophonemic rules.

If we examine the PAST element, we will note that all English verbs fall into two classes: those that form the past with [d], [t] or [ɨd]—which we will call Verb$_1$, and those which do not—which we will call Verb$_2$. Looking closely at the verbs in Verb$_1$, we will note that the pattern of [d:t:ɨd] is quite clear: Verbs in Verb$_1$ ending in a vowel or a voiced consonant (except [d]), take [d]; those ending in a voiceless consonant except [t], take [t]; those ending in [t] or [d], take [ɨd]. These facts may be expressed by the following morphophonemic rules:

M.1. Verb$_1$ ends in $\begin{cases} \text{vowel} \\ \text{voiced consonant except } [d] \end{cases}$ + PAST →

Verb$_1$ ends in $\begin{cases} \text{vowel} \\ \text{voiced consonant except } [d] \end{cases}$ + [d]

M.2. Verb$_1$ ends in voiceless consonant except [t] + PAST →
Verb$_1$ ends in voiceless consonant except [t] + [t]

M.3. Verb$_1$ ends in [t] or [d] + PAST → Verb$_1$ ending in [t] or [d] + [ɨd]

These rules may be collapsed into the single morphophonemic rule:

M.4. Verb$_1$ ending in $\begin{bmatrix} \begin{cases} \text{vowel} \\ \text{voiced consonant except } [d] \end{cases} \\ \text{voiceless consonant except } [t] \\ [t] \text{ or } [d] \end{bmatrix}$ + PAST →

Verb$_1$ ending in $\begin{bmatrix} \begin{cases} \text{vowel} \\ \text{voiced consonant except } [d] \end{cases} \\ \text{voiceless consonant except } [t] \\ [t] \text{ or } [d] \end{bmatrix} + \begin{bmatrix} [d] \\ [t] \\ [ɨd] \end{bmatrix}$

Here the large square brackets indicate that if the symbols in a given position on one side of the plus sign are chosen, then the symbols in the corresponding position on the other side of the plus must also be chosen; i.e., if the top symbol is selected on the left, then the top symbol must also be selected on the right.

Another example of morphophonemic rules involves English plurals. In Chapter Two we gave a series of rules for the distribution of [s], [z] and [ɨz] as the PLURAL element. We can now restate these rules in terms of rewrite rules.

M.5. N_1 ending in $\begin{bmatrix} \begin{cases} \text{vowel} \\ \text{voiced consonant except } [z\ ž\ j] \\ \text{voiceless consonant except } [s\ š\ č] \end{cases} \\ [s\ š\ č\ z\ ž\ j] \end{bmatrix}$ $+$ PLURAL

N_1 ending in $\begin{bmatrix} \begin{cases} \text{vowel} \\ \text{voiced consonant except } [z\ ž\ j] \\ \text{voiceless consonant except } [s\ š\ č] \end{cases} \\ [s\ š\ č\ z\ ž\ j] \end{bmatrix}$ $+$ $\begin{bmatrix} [z] \\ [s] \\ [ɨz] \end{bmatrix}$

Here, N_1 means a noun which has a plural like that of **dogs, hats** or **roses,** nouns taking plurals like **men, geese, mice, sheep, phenomena** would be covered by other morphophonemic rules.

A final example of morphophonemic rules is that of the indefinite article. The indefinite article has two forms, **a** and **an.** In the surface tree of a derived NP like:

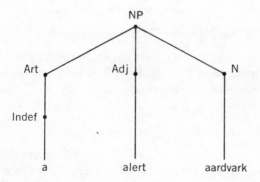

a morphophonemic rule changes the article **a** to **an.** This rule operates whenever the article is followed by a noun beginning with a vowel or by an adjective beginning with a vowel. The rule may be formalized as:

M.6. **a** $+ \begin{cases} \text{adj. beginning with vowel} \\ \text{noun beginning with vowel} \end{cases} \rightarrow$

an $+ \begin{cases} \text{adj. beginning with vowel} \\ \text{noun beginning with vowel} \end{cases}$

From M.1–M.6 it can be seen that morphophonemic rules operate on surface structures. The outputs of these rules are the phonological representations of surface structures. In Chapter Four we will look at one way of viewing these phonological representations.

Environments

At the beginning of this chapter it was mentioned that there are both "anywhere rules" and context-sensitive rules. The morphophonemic rules just discussed are excellent examples of context-sensitive rules, for they require the enumeration of the environments in which they occur. Occasionally, however, it is desirable to reduce a rule like M.6 yet further, and so the symbol:

/_____

has been introduced. This may be read as "in the environment" or, simply "in env." Rather than explain at length, let us merely rewrite M.6 using this symbol:

M.6a. $a \rightarrow an$ /_____ $\#$ $\begin{cases} \text{adj. beginning with vowel} \\ \text{noun beginning with vowel} \end{cases}$

Where $\#$ means "word boundary." The rule thus reads:

M.6b. Rewrite **a** as **an** when it occurs before an adjective or a noun beginning with a vowel. There is a word boundary between **a/an** and the following noun/adj.

Rewriting some problems

In Chapters One and Two we looked at some typical problems in descriptive phonology and morphology. Let us now look at them in terms of the various types of rules discussed in Chapter Three.

Let us look first at the Totonac problem at the end of Chapter One. We then saw that [ḁ i̥ u̥] occurred finally and that [a i u] occurred elsewhere. We can now rephrase this conclusion as:

$$\begin{bmatrix} a \\ i \\ u \end{bmatrix} \rightarrow \begin{bmatrix} \overset{\circ}{a} \\ \overset{\circ}{i} \\ \overset{\circ}{u} \end{bmatrix} / \underline{\hspace{1cm}} \#$$

This rule states that [a i u] are rewritten as [ḁ i̥ u̥] before a word boundary.

Let us now look at the Luganda problem at the end of Chapter Two. It might seem as though we could set up the rules:

$$\begin{bmatrix} omu \\ omu \\ olu \\ eki \end{bmatrix} + \text{noun stem} \rightarrow \begin{bmatrix} aba \\ emi \\ en \\ ebi \end{bmatrix} + \text{noun stem}$$

and:

noun stem → { **-kazi, -sawo, sika, -lenzi, -ti, -dumu,**
-sumaali, -naku, -senyi, -ntu, -bbo, etc. }

But this will not work. How would someone know whether **omukazi** was to be pluralized as **abakasi** or *__emikasi__? How would they know that the plural of **omuti** was **emiti** and not *__abati__? Try to formulate a set of rules (or a rule) which will enable you to correctly pluralize the Lugandan nouns given in Chapter Two.

FOUR

Features

Phonological features

At the end of the preceding chapter several linguistic phenomena were rewritten as rules. It must be apparent that not only such items as the English indefinite article but all morphophonemic rules can be simplified in various ways. For example, in German, which has two slit fricatives [x] and [ç] (the former velar, the latter palatal), we can construct a rule to demonstrate their distribution. Such a rule would be of the form:

M.8. **ch** → $\begin{cases} [ç] \text{ / front vowel \_\_\_\_\_} \\ [x] \text{ / mid or back vowel \_\_\_\_\_} \end{cases}$

This accounts for the fact that **Bücher** and **ich** are pronounced with [ç] **ach** and **Loch** have [x].

In Spanish, where intervocalic [b] becomes a fricative, we could specify something like:

M.9. $[b] \to [v]$ / V___V   (V = any vowel)

or:

M.9a. voiced bilabial stop → voiced bilabial fricative / V___V

M.9 and M.9a account for the pronunciation of such words as **Cuba** and **caballo,** with medial [v].

Unfortunately, the list of symbols given in Chapter One is insufficient for the myriad speech sounds of the several thousand languages of the world. M.8 and M.9 have introduced three additional symbols, for example. Moreover, no one ever pronounces the same sound in exactly the same way, and so an attempt at real one-sound, one-sign symbolization leads us to an infinite number of symbols. We can eliminate some of these sounds (and symbols) by confining our interests to "relevant" or "distinctive" speech sounds. But this still leaves us with a vast number of symbols. Using such descriptions as those in M.9a is less than satisfactory, because there is much information (direction of air flow, tongue contour, etc.) which is not given. A first attempt at establishing a set of criteria which would account for all language sounds as a series of matrices of binary distinctions was formulated by Roman Jakobson, C. Gunnar M. Fant, and Morris Halle in 1951. Since then the original list of determiners—or **distinctive features**—has been extensively revised and elaborated. One such revision was suggested by James D. McCawley in the autumn of 1967. The one we will use is that of **The Sound Pattern of English** by Noam Chomsky and Morris Halle (1968). The final list of features used by Chomsky and Halle is:

Major class features
  Sonorant
  Vocalic
  Consonantal
Cavity features
  Coronal
  Anterior
  Tongue-body features
    High
    Low
    Back
  Round
  Distributed
  Covered
  Glottal Constriction
  Secondary apertures
    Nasal
    Lateral
Manner of articulation features
  Continuant
  Release features

        Primary release
        Secondary release
      Supplementary movements
      Suction
          Velaric suction (clicks)
          Implosion
      Pressure
          Velaric pressure
          Ejectives
      Tense
  Source features
      Heightened subglottal pressure
      Voice
      Strident
  Prosodic features
      Stress
      Pitch
          High
          Low
          Elevated
          Rising
          Falling
          Concave
      Length

Of these, in addition to the prosodic features (which we will not discuss in this book), only thirteen are needed to describe English: vocalic, consonantal, high, back, low, anterior, coronal, round, tense, voice, continuant, nasal, strident. As mentioned above, each of these features encompasses itself and its opposite (e.g., + consonantal and − consonantal). The definitions of the features are as follows:

Vocalic sounds are produced with an oral cavity in which the most radical constriction does not exceed that found in the high vowels [i] and [u] (i.e., vocalic sounds are voiced vowels and liquids);

Consonantal sounds are produced with a radical obstruction in the midsaggital region of the vocal tract;

High sounds are produced by raising the body of the tongue above the level that it occupies in neutral position;

Back sounds are produced by retracting the body of the tongue from the neutral position;

Low sounds are produced by lowering the body of the tongue below the level it occupies in neutral position;

Anterior sounds are produced with an obstruction located in front of the palato-alveolar region of the mouth;

Coronal sounds are produced with the blade of the tongue raised from neutral position;

Rounded sounds are produced with a narrowing of the lip orifice;

Tense sounds are produced with considerably more muscular effort than are − Tense (or **Lax**) sounds;

Voiced sounds are produced by vibration of the vocal cords;

Continuant sounds do not block the air flow completely at any point (− Continuants are **Stops**);

Nasal sounds are produced with a lowered velum;

Strident sounds are marked acoustically by greater noisiness than their non-strident counterparts.

Using these features, the English consonants and vowels of Chapter One may be represented as in the overleaf chart on page 42.

Using this sort of feature system, we might now once more rewrite our solution to the Totonac problem of Chapter One as:

$$\begin{bmatrix} + \text{ vocalic} \\ - \text{ consonantal} \\ + \text{ voice} \end{bmatrix} \longrightarrow \begin{bmatrix} + \text{ vocalic} \\ - \text{ consonantal} \\ - \text{ voice} \end{bmatrix} / \underline{\quad} \#$$

As we have no consonants in final position in our Totonac, we might merely write:

$$[+ \text{ voice}] \longrightarrow [- \text{ voice}] / \underline{\quad} \#$$

which is valid for our brief corpus. This description is obviously much simpler.

Noun features

If you look at two sentences like:

1. The boy laughed.
2. The airplane laughed.

it is immediately apparent that something is wrong with the second sentence. We don't ordinarily think of an airplane as capable of laugh-

	ɨ	ɨH	i	u	e	ə	o	æ	y	w	r	l	p	b	f	v	m	t	d	θ	ð	n	s	z	č	ǰ	š	ž	k	g	ŋ	h
vocalic	+	+	+	+	+	+	+	+	−	−	+	+	−	−	−	−	−	−	−	−	−	−	−	−	−	−	−	−	−	−	−	−
consonantal	−	−	−	−	−	−	−	−	−	−	+	+	+	+	+	+	+	+	+	+	+	+	+	+	+	+	+	+	+	+	+	−
high	+	+	+	+	−	−	−	−	+	+	−	−	−	−	−	−	−	−	−	−	−	−	−	−	+	+	+	+	+	+	+	−
back	+	+	−	+	−	+	+	−	−	+	−	−	−	−	−	−	−	−	−	−	−	−	−	−	−	−	−	−	+	+	+	−
low	−	−	−	−	−	−	−	+	−	−																						
anterior											+	+	+	+	+	+	+	+	+	+	+	+	+	+	−	−	−	−	−	−	−	−
coronal											+	+	−	−	−	−	−	+	+	+	+	+	+	+	+	+	+	+	−	−	−	−
round	−	−	−	+	−	−	+	−	−	+																						
tense	−	+	+	+	+	−	+	−	−	−																						
voice											+	+	−	+	−	+	+	−	+	−	+	+	−	+	−	+	−	+	−	+	+	−
continuant											+	+	−	−	+	+	−	−	−	+	+	−	+	+	−	−	+	+	−	−	−	+
nasal											−	−	−	−	−	−	+	−	−	−	−	+	−	−	−	−	−	−	−	−	+	−
strident											−	−	−	−	+	+	−	−	−	−	−	−	+	+	+	+	+	+	−	−	−	−

ter. In fact, nouns like **boy** and **airplane** belong to different categories of nouns. We can categorize noun types in terms of features, much as we can phonological phenomena. For example, we might view part of the matrix for **boy** as:

$$\begin{bmatrix} + \text{ N} \\ + \text{ animate} \end{bmatrix}$$

whereas the similar portion of the matrix for **airplane** would be:

$$\begin{bmatrix} + \text{ N} \\ - \text{ animate} \end{bmatrix}$$

In addition to being either animate or inanimate, nouns may be common or proper (+ or − common), human or non-human (+ or − human), concrete or abstract (+ or − concrete)

Occasionally, one feature may subsume another in some way. Thus, if a noun is − concrete, there is no point in stating that it is also − animate and − human, for no abstract noun (like **happiness** or **death**) can be animate, and no inanimate noun can be human. On the other hand, positives must be stated, for dogs are just as concrete and animate as women, but they are not + human.

Troilus, for example, is:

$$\begin{bmatrix} + \text{ N} \\ - \text{ common} \\ + \text{ concrete} \\ + \text{ animate} \\ + \text{ human} \end{bmatrix}$$

whereas **horse** is:

$$\begin{bmatrix} + \text{ N} \\ + \text{ common} \\ + \text{ concrete} \\ + \text{ animate} \\ - \text{ human} \end{bmatrix}$$

and **Illinois** is:

$$\begin{bmatrix} + \text{ N} \\ - \text{ common} \\ + \text{ concrete} \\ - \text{ animate} \end{bmatrix}$$

There are other features which the noun has in the deep structure. For example, it may be $+$ or $-$ singular ($-$ singular is the same as plural) or it may be $+$ or $-$ definite. The article is the best way of telling from the surface structure whether a noun is $+$ or $-$ definite. If the noun is $+$ definite, it will be preceded by **the;** if the noun is $-$ definite, it will be preceded by **a/an.** As we can indicate plurality and definiteness in the feature matrix of a noun, we need not indicate it in the deep structure of the sentence. What we have in place of this is a transformation, for example, which inserts the correct article or adds the plural **-s** (the morphophonemic rules will alter the plural to its proper form).

The NP **the boys** thus has a tree like:

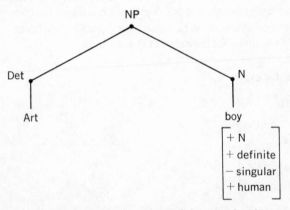

The feature $+$ definite means that the article must be **the;** $-$ singular means that the noun will be read as boy $+$ s, and that at another level a morphophonemic rule will rewrite this **s** as [z].

Pronouns also have features which become important on the deep structure level. English differentiates between the object form of a pronoun and the subject form of a pronoun, i.e. it differentiates between **I** and **me** or **he** and **him.** We refer to this feature as $+$ or $-$ accusative. We also differentiate between person categories in the pronoun. **I** is thus + first person, or + I; **you** is + II; and **he, she** or **it** are + III. Finally, English has sex differentiated pronouns in **he** and **she.** We consider this last feature as + or − male.

Our deep structure tree no longer has such forms as **me** or **him.** Only − accusatives occur in the deep structure. The tree for **Sally loves him** is thus:

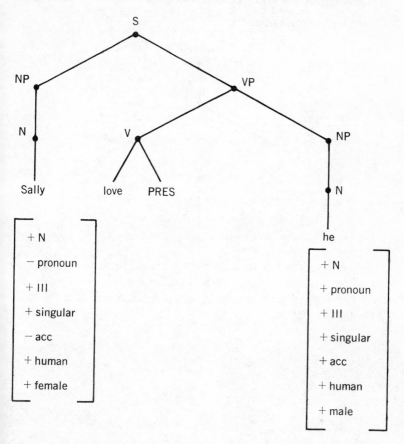

Ultimately, our set of matrices ought to be able to distinguish lexical items from one another up to the level of stylistic variation. In terms of features even homonyms are easily distinguishable, as has been shown by J. J. Katz and J. A. Fodor.

If we take a word like **bachelor,** we will note that there are four main entries under this heading in most dictionaries, and that each of these entries has a "definition" much like one of the following:

1. a man who has never married;
2. a young knight serving under the standard of another knight;
3. a man or woman who holds the first or lowest academic degree;
4. a young fur seal without a mate during breeding time.

These may be set on a tree like:

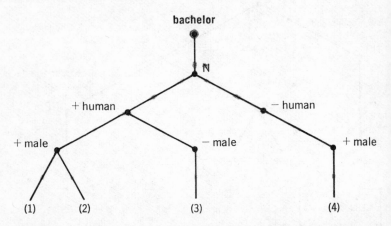

Neither phonological nor grammatical nor semantic feature systems are perfect, and certainly semantic features are less perfect than the other two, but the basic concept is unimpeachable, and so is the utility of the feature matrix.

FIVE

Diachronic and synchronic linguistics

All of the language phenomena examined in the first four chapters have been **synchronic,** that is, we have concerned ourselves with that which is actually happening in the language as it is spoken today. Our statements about English have concerned the spoken language of the mid-twentieth century. However, language can be viewed as a historical phenomenon, and the development of a language or group of languages over centuries and millennia may be examined. This study is called **diachronic** linguistics, the study of language through time.

It is important that we not confuse synchronic and diachronic phenomena, for while we would hope that someday we would have a set of synchronic grammars for, say, every level of the development of English from the time of King Alfred to the present, and that these synchronic grammars be compatible enough so that we could trace each individual phenomenon from stage to stage, this is far from the case at present. Were this true, however, we could view historical linguistics as a field which assembled all of the synchronic grammars in a pile and then did a cross-section of the grammars, a real slice through time.

Just as earlier twentieth century linguists devoted most of their time to collection of surface phenomena, so the nineteenth century

47

linguists (with the sole exception of Wilhelm von Humboldt) devoted themselves to tracing historical phenomena and collating comparative information. It was as a result of this work that the various members of the Indo-European family of languages were identified and their relationships—to a large extent—traced, collated, and reported.

The most familiar example of this is the so-called "first consonantal shift" of Germanic, discovered by R. C. Rask and formulated by Jacob Grimm (therefore frequently called Grimm's Law). This shift involved the initial sounds of such words as **father, horn,** and **thin.** It was noted that the Latin (and Greek in many cases) equivalents of these words had voiceless stops, **p (pater), k (cornu), t (tenuis).** Similarly, the initial sound of **tooth** and the no-longer-pronounced **k** of **knee** corresponded to voiced stops in Latin **(dens** and **genu).** Other correspondences involved the initials of **brother,** and **comb.** From this and other data, Grimm formulated the rule that the correspondences between the Germanic languages (German, English, Dutch, and the Scandinavian dialects) and the other related languages (the members of the "Indo-European" family) were such that the following correspondences could be set up:

IE	Germanic
[p	f
t	θ
k	x, h
b	p
d	t
g	k
bh	b
dh	d
gh	g]

and that these correspondences involved changes (or a "shift") on the part of the Germanic languages.

Comparative work among the various Indo-European languages led to several attempts at reconstructing the "parent language" from which the historically recorded and modern dialects were descended. Most of this work was done on an *ad hoc* basis: that is, each time phenomena were noticed, a new law or development or sound shift was made up to satisfy the data. There were no attempts at organizing systems or at ordering most of the changes. Some ordering was done where it was either obvious or necessary for shift A to have occurred before shift B, but even here the results were for the most part limited and lacked any sort of rigor.

Within the past two decades several attempts have been undertaken at making historical and comparative linguistics "more scientific." One of the systems devised, called **lexicostatistics** or **glottochronology** has had some lasting effect.

The basic purpose of lexicostatistics is to determine on the basis of common vocabulary (that is, words which are similar, like Tagalog [pīliʔ], Javanese [pilik], and Batak [pili], all of which mean 'choose') the degree of relationship. Without going into the mathematics, it was found, by comparison of several languages where the history was actually known, that vocabulary loss (and innovation) occurs at a fairly constant rate. Lists were then made up of "basic" items and, using these basic word lists, attempts were made at dating the split between two languages. That is, given that German, English, Latin, Greek, Russian, and Armenian have a common ancestor, how long ago were English and German mutually comprehensible dialects? how long ago were the ancestors of English and Russian mutually comprehensible? etc. While the actual attempts at dating have met with varying degrees of success, the evaluation of degrees of relationship on the basis of common vocabulary has been more effective. Let us imagine four languages, A, B, C, and D. Using the 250-word list, it is found that A and B share 60 percent of their vocabulary, A and C share 40 percent, and A and D share 45 percent. Further, B and C share 50 percent and B and D share 20 percent; C and D share 60 percent. On the first glance, we can say that A and B and C and D are closer to one another than any of the other pairings. If we postulate a parent language X, we can thus construct a tree like:

to represent the relationships.

The use of phrase structure rules to represent historical phenomena has also proven of value in the last five years or so. Several "laws" revealed by nineteenth-century linguists have been shown to be invalid or, in some cases, to have very diverse implications. Rather than go into great detail, we will here give rules for some of the historical phonology of Old Icelandic (these rules are from James E. Cathey's **Relative Chronology of Old Icelandic Phonology,** University of Washington dissertation, 1967).

1. In Old Icelandic, nasal consonants are assimilated to voiceless stops:

$$\text{m, n, ŋ} \longrightarrow \begin{bmatrix} p \\ t \\ k \end{bmatrix} / \underline{\hspace{1cm}} \begin{bmatrix} p \\ t \\ k \end{bmatrix}$$

or:

$$\begin{bmatrix} - \text{ vocalic} \\ + \text{ consonantal} \\ + \text{ nasal} \end{bmatrix} \longrightarrow \begin{bmatrix} - \text{ vocalic} \\ + \text{ consonantal} \\ - \text{ nasal} \\ - \text{ continuant} \\ - \text{ voice} \\ \alpha \text{ feature} \end{bmatrix} / \underline{\hspace{1cm}} \begin{bmatrix} - \text{ vocalic} \\ + \text{ consonantal} \\ - \text{ nasal} \\ - \text{ continuant} \\ - \text{ voice} \\ \alpha \text{ feature} \end{bmatrix}$$

where "α feature" means that all the other features are identical.

2. [d] becomes [ð] after [r] in Old Icelandic:

$$\text{d} \longrightarrow \text{ð} / [\text{r}] \underline{\hspace{1cm}}$$

or:

$$[- \text{ continuant}] \longrightarrow [+ \text{ continuant}] / \begin{bmatrix} + \text{ vocalic} \\ + \text{ consonantal} \\ - \text{ anterior} \\ + \text{ coronal} \end{bmatrix} \underline{\hspace{1cm}}$$

As can be seen in much recent work in generative phonology (especially that of Joseph B. Voyles of the University of Washington and that of his students), many problems of linguistic history can be solved by setting up sets of ordered rules. The basic assumption of this method is that the philosophic tenet known as Occam's Razor is valid. If there are several possible solutions to a problem, the simplest one is most probable; if there are several possible orderings or descriptions which satisfy an observed phenomenon, the one involving the fewest steps or the fewest symbols, or the one offering the greatest degree of generalization about the language or Language in general is the closest to what actually happened.

Language and thought

Noam Chomsky has called linguistics a "particular branch of cognitive psychology," and while this is bound to shock and horrify most traditional linguists, it contains a good deal of validity. "Mentalism" was an imprecation for most descriptivists, but Chomsky and a number of other linguists have shown that in the deepest sense of the word, linguistics must be mentalistic as it seeks to discover the mental reality underlying the actual performance of a speaker. It is most likely an exaggeration to say that the phrase structure rules, the transformational rules, and the morphophonemic rules actually duplicate what is going on in the human mind (another "school" of linguistics, the stratificationalists, make precisely this claim—that stratificational grammar replicates the neural responses of the mind—but we shall leave such grandiose claims to the darkness they so well deserve). However, it is an attempt at duplicating—or at least representing—the processes which seem to make up sentence-formation and sentence-comprehension. A number of recent psychological research projects in the areas of language learning and verbal behavior seem to indicate that the notions inherent in transformational-generative grammar have at least some degree of validity.

In constructing a description of language, there are several basic ideas which must be examined. The first of these is the distinction between competence and performance.

Performance deals with the actual verbal behavior of a speaker. A description of a speaker's performance will have to deal with innumerable false starts, hesitations, incomplete utterances. Most of these phenomena, interesting as they may be for some psychologists, are of no real importance where the language of the speaker is concerned; the speaker "knows" that he "makes mistakes" when he speaks. On the other hand, the **competence** of a speaker involves his being able to distinguish an utterance from a non-utterance in his native tongue. For example, given:

1. It's hot, and it's raining, too.
2. It's hot, and it's raining, either.
3. It's hot, and it's not nice, too.
4. It's hot, and it's not nice, either.

every native speaker of English will mark sentences 2 and 3 as "ungrammatical." Sentences 1 and 4 are acceptable. Furthermore, every native speaker of English can understand a sentence like:

5. Seventeen magenta marine mollusks engulfed
   the sleeping sloth.

despite the fact that the odds are very good no one reading it has ever seen it before. Every day most people say things they have never said before and understand things they have never heard before. They can do these things because they have mastered the phrase structure and transformational rules of English. Moreover, they have not learned these rules explicitly, but have abstracted them from the data presented to them almost from the moment of birth.

This leads us to the other contention inherent in the transformational-generative approach to grammar: the notion of **language universals.** The notion of such universals was briefly noted in the Introduction, but now we will view it more extensively.

In the seventeenth and eighteenth centuries, there originated a split among philosophers. This split concerned the question of whether a child was born with certain innate faculties or whether the child was a blank slate—a *tabula rasa*—upon which everything had to be imposed. The champions of innate ideas were called Rationalists (their most famous proponents were Descartes, Arnauld, and the Port Royal grammarians); those who thought of the child as a blank slate were called Empiricists (the most famous proponent of this was Locke). The notion of whether or not a child is a complete blank at birth is important to psychologists and educators, but it is also of great importance to linguists.

If a child is a blank slate, then the notion of deep structure is untenable. Only if every human being possesses some sort of language faculty at birth, does the idea of deep structure become viable. Luckily, our experience seems to indicate that language is not merely a learned habit. If it were a habit, if all we did was to take apart the sentences we have heard (from earliest childhood) and rearrange them, then how could we possibly produce sentences we have never heard before? And, moreover, how could we comprehend sentences we have never heard before? It is doubtful whether anyone reading this had ever read a sentence like sentence 5 before, yet it is completely intelligible, as is one like:

6. Hemicellulose is one of a series of polysaccharides
   easily hydrolyzable into simple sugars.

even though many of the words in sentence 6 are probably unfamiliar.

It would seem that from earliest childhood infants somehow abstract data from the sentences they hear, and that by the age of six or eight every child has somehow abstracted all the phrase structure rules and transformational rules of his language. This is not to say that a six- or eight-year-old is completely competent in his language, nor that his language will not change as he grows. What we are claiming is that by the time a child enters second or third grade he has mastered all the rules of his language community. He may add vocabulary—hopefully he will—as it would be difficult for an adult to manage with a six-year-old's vocabulary; he may even add a few syntactic rules (one which permits addition of clauses to sentences); but by and large the child of six or eight has a grammar, and his grammar is that of the language community in which he lives.

Returning now to several statements in the Introduction to this book, it can be seen why creativity is of such importance. For if there is the possibility for creation of utterances and the comprehension of such utterances—if, in other words, each of us can pronounce sentences we have never heard before and understand innovative sentences—then the basic concepts of transformational-generative grammar are valid: there is a finite set of rules underlying the infinite set of sentences of a language, and this finite set of rules is mastered by every native speaker of that language at a very early age.

SEVEN

Some areas of linguistics

Anthropological linguistics

Anthropology is a rather broad discipline, embracing, as it does, any subject matter connected with man and his activities: aspects of economics, linguistics, literature, music, art, archaeology, and diet are all part of anthropology. Further, we can divide anthropology into two large areas: cultural anthropology and physical anthropology. The second of these deals with the classification of humans on the basis of physical structure (skeleton, musculature) and the comparison of these physical structures with those of the apes. Anthropological linguistics is a branch of cultural anthropology.

Field work—the transcription and analysis of a natural language using a native informant in his own habitat—is one of the most important areas of anthropological linguistics. Here the modern tape recorder may prove to be the linguist's most important tool. Unfortunately, almost all work in this area deals with surface phenomena, and little attempt has been made to establish confirmation of hypotheses or establishment of significant generalizations on the basis of data obtained from or through anthropologists.

Cultural anthropology has broadened our horizons, so that we no longer view Western Europe and North America as "standard" and the rest of the world as "curious." We have become more urbane and less chauvinistic. Even the traditional descriptivist does not require some newly discovered language of Central Africa or Indonesia to fit the pattern of the grammatical categories of Latin or Greek. Unfortunately, little work has been done on the basic similarities of all language phenomena (as opposed to the contrasts between them) save on the lines indicated in Chapters Three and Four.

The questions of language and culture and language universals come in here, too. Though there is much that could be said further about language universals, we shall merely remark here that if—as seems likely—all of mankind possess an innate language faculty, and if all languages have the same deep structures (differing only in lexicons, transformations, phonologies), as von Humboldt claimed in 1835 and transformational grammarians have maintained over the past decade, then there must be "deep structure" similarities to be found in other of man's behavioral patterns, and that this would be of primary importance to anthropologists. Lévi-Strauss's attempts at finding "deep structure" phenomena in the mythic themes of mankind are gestures in this direction.

The question of language and culture has long been a fascinating one. Basically, it boils down to whether or not the language—or the structure of a language—forces the thought of the culture using that language in certain specific directions. For example, given a language like Bassa (Liberia) which divides up the spectrum into two parts **hui** (equivalent to our **purple, blue,** and **green**) and **zinza** (equivalent to our **yellow, orange,** and **red**), we may find that it permits greater generalization concerning some phenomena (here, botanical flower-colors, where American botanists have had to invent **xanthic** and **cyanic** for just these areas of the spectrum). It must be pointed out that such divisions have nothing to do with "seeing" the difference between say **lavender** and **aquamarine,** but merely concern the basic division of the spectrum. It seems that while the language used does have some influence on the conceptualization of certain things within a culture, every known language borrows or coins new items for its lexicon with ease whenever the vocabulary is found wanting.

Sociolinguistics

As might be guessed from the word, sociolinguistics deals with the sociological applications of linguistic data and the linguistic uses of sociological data. India, Belgium, and Canada show in their language and social problems the importance of one of these areas to the other; and the change in social structure has brought with it an interesting change in kinship terminology in the Soviet Union over the past half century. Furthermore, though all of us are conscious of geographical dialects (e.g., North and South Germany, "southern" [actually south-eastern] American English, and New England English), there has been little awareness of the importance of social dialects.

A beginning was made at studying social dialects by William Labov in his brilliant **Social Stratification of English in New York City** a few years ago, but there is much work still to be done.

Another area of sociolinguistics is that of multilingualism. It has been shown that the factors influencing language choice in the Philippines make up a valuable description of the problems which develop in inter-personal relations among multilingual speakers.

It is difficult to attempt enumeration of the many possible areas of sociolinguistics, and so we will merely stop with the assertion that it is the study of the interactions of language and society.

Psycholinguistics

Most psychologists are aware of the fact that the human mind operates on linguistic symbols. Similarly, most linguists have always admitted that some sort of psychological drive must set the grammatical process into motion. The interaction of these attitudes is the area of **psycholinguistics.**

Two types of psychologists have interested themselves in linguistics: the behavioral psychologists, who have tried to replace thought with speech—moving from an intangible to a physical manifestation. They refer to speech as "verbal behavior." This branch of psychological-linguistic inquiry has proven largely sterile. The other branch of psychology interested in language is cognitive psychology. In particular, the cognitive psychologists have been interested in the "psychological processes" involved in sentence production and sentence recognition. In line with this, they have also been interested in the child's learning of language, in his acquisition, for example, of the morphophonemic rules for forming the plural or the past.

Another area of interest to the psychologist is the degree of deviation from the norm that is still acceptable to the speaker and hearer. Here it becomes obvious that there are degrees of grammaticality:

that some sentences are more acceptable than others, though all o'
this set may be "ungrammatical" in some way. Thus, we can say that:

    1. *He am one of the nicest guys I know.

or:

    2. *We didn't go there, too.

are less ungrammatical (or more grammatical) than are:

    3. **They the seven book reading through too is.

or:

    4. **Description of the these I phrased phenomena are.

Finally, there is much work to be done in the area of perception and
cognition. Just how we perceive a sound or a syllable; just what it is in a
feature matrix that conveys the information in the final analysis; jus'
how facial and hand gestures amplify (and in some cases reverse) the
content of an utterance—all are problems which concern the psycho-
linguist. And they are problems, the solution of which would be of grea'
interest to scholars and teachers in all areas of knowledge.

Other areas

There are a number of other specific areas in linguistics, but we shal'
not even attempt to enumerate them all here. However, several area:
deserve mention, despite their apparent disregard. The first of these i:
semantics, the study of meaning. In this area much work has beer
done. As late as twenty years ago many linguists scorned meaning a'
irrelevant to linguistic analysis. Recent research has shown that it is o'
great importance, though the exact place of semantics in a transfor
mational-generative grammar is still uncertain.

Another area lies on the borderline between linguistics and philos
ophy, and is usually called the philosophy of language. This field i
concerned with the formal and theoretical problems which are the
consequence of contemporary linguistic theory.

Fields like **lexicography**—the writing of dictionaries—and **dialectol
ogy**—the study of (usually regional) dialects—seem to be basically dat:
collection, and will therefore not be covered here.

Finally, linguistics in general, and transformational-generative gram mar and psycholinguistics in particular, can be of great value to the theory and practice of **modern language teaching**—both foreign language and primary language instruction. The instruction of the physically and psychologically handicapped (physiological and psychological speech and hearing disorders and the therapy for such disorders) may be considered a subclass of primary language teaching.

Selected bibliography

Introduction

obins, R. H. **A short History of Linguistics.** Bloomington: Indiana University Press, 1968.

alus, Peter H., ed. **On Language: Plato to von Humboldt.** New York: Holt, Rinehart and Winston, 1969.

Chapters One and Two

loomfield, Leonard. **Language.** New York: Holt, 1933.

leason, H. A., Jr. **An Introduction to Descriptive Linguistics.** Rev. ed. New York: Holt, Rinehart and Winston, 1961.

adefoged, Peter. **Elements of Acoustic Phonetics.** Chicago: University of Chicago Press, 1962.

ostal, Paul. **Constituent Structure: A Study of the Contemporary Models of Syntactic Description.** 2nd ed. Bloomington: Indiana University Research Center in Anthropology, Folklore and Linguistics, 1967.

Chapter Three

homsky, Noam. **Aspects of the Theory of Syntax.** Cambridge: Massachusetts Institute of Technology Press, 1965.

————. "Current Issues in Linguistic Theory." **Janua Linguarum** N 38. The Hague: Mouton and Co., 1964.

————, "Syntactic Structures." **Janua Linguarum** No. 4. The Hagu Mouton and Co., 1957.

Jacobs, Roderick A., and Peter S. Rosenbaum. **Grammar 1** and **Gram mar 2.** Boston: Ginn and Co., 1967.

Katz, Jerrold J., and Paul M. Postal. **An Integrated Theory of Linguisti Descriptions.** Cambridge: Massachusetts Institute of Technolog Press, 1964.

Chapter Four

Chomsky, Noam, and Morris Halle. **The Sound Pattern of English.** Ne York: Harper and Row, 1968.

Jakobson, Roman, C. Gunnar M. Fant, and Morris Halle. **Preliminarie to Speech Analysis: The Distinctive Features and their Correlate** Cambridge: Massachusetts Institute of Technology Press, 195 seventh printing, 1967.

————, and Morris Halle. "Fundamentals of Language." **Janua Li guarum** No. 1. The Hague: Mouton and Co., 1956.

Postal, Paul M. **Aspects of Phonological Theory.** New York: Harper ar Row, 1968.

Chapter Five

de Saussure, Ferdinand. **Course in General Linguistics,** translated Wade Baskin. New York: Philosophical Library, 1959.

Lehmann, Winfred P. **Historical Linguistics: An Introduction.** New Yor Holt, Rinehart and Winston, 1962.

Chapter Six

Carroll, John B. **Language and Thought.** Englewood Cliffs: Prentic Hall, 1964.

Chomsky, Noam. **Language and Mind.** New York: Harcourt, Brace a World, 1968.

Greenberg, Joseph H., ed. **Universals of Language.** Cambridge: Ma sachusetts Institute of Technology Press, 1963.

Smith, Frank, and George A. Miller, eds. **The Genesis of Languag** Cambridge: Massachusetts Institute of Technology Press, 1966.

Chapter Seven

Austin, J. L. **How to Do Things with Words.** Edited by J. O. Urmson. New York: Oxford University Press, 1965.

Fodor, Jerry A., and Jerrold J. Katz, eds. **The Structure of Language: Readings in the Philosophy of Language.** Englewood Cliffs: Prentice-Hall, 1964.

Katz, Jerrold J. **The Philosophy of Language.** New York: Harper and Row, 1966.

Labov, William. **The Social Stratification of English in New York City.** Washington: Center for Applied Linguistics, 1966.

Lieberson, Stanley, ed. "Explorations in Sociolinguistics." **IJAL** Vol. 33, No. 4, Part II, 1967.

Osgood, Charles E., and Thomas A. Sebeok, eds. **Psycholinguistics.** Bloomington: Indiana University Press, 1965.

Samarin, William J. **Field Linguistics.** New York: Holt, Rinehart and Winston, 1967.

Saporta, Sol, ed. **Psycholinguistics: A Book of Readings.** New York: Holt, Rinehart and Winston, 1961.

Some Linguistics Journals

The most important linguistics journals in the United States are **Language,** the journal of the Linguistic Society of America, and **IJAL,** the **International Journal of American Linguistics;** in special areas, **Anthropological Linguistics, JAOS** (the **Journal of the American Oriental Society**), the **Journal of Speech and Hearing Research,** and **JEGP** (the **Journal of English and Germanic Philology**) are of interest.

The **Journal of Linguistics, Linguistics, Foundations of Language, Orbis,** and **Indogermanische Forschungen** are among the most important European journals, though there are many more.

The proceedings of the various International Congresses are also valuable. The last two (the Ninth, held in Cambridge, Massachusetts, in 1962 and the Tenth, held in Bucharest, Romania, in 1967) produced many papers of extraordinary interest.

The most important bibliographical source in linguistics is the **Bibliographie Linguistique/Linguistic Bibliography** published annually, save for the two composite volumes for the decade preceding 1947.

Index